ANOTHER SPRINGTIME

The Poetry of Life

SALLY M. HARRIS

ISBN- 979-8-218-19808-4

Acknowledgments

A special thank you to my husband, Al Harris, for editing and formatting assistance.
I dedicate this book to my family and friends.
Life is rich because of you.

Table of Contents

Word Play

A poet's
Words are
Butterfly wings
Of light

Set free
To explore
With curious intent

Pausing to rest
On each hilltop of Truth
Sometimes finding kindred souls
Basking there

Nothing in the world
Makes a heart sing
Like that.

Summer's Child

Looking back, I remember
The cottonwoods rustling
Sweetening the hot summer air

Skipping down the sizzling sidewalk
Holding Mother's hand
Feeling her warmth and her wedding band

She sang a simple tune
Swinging my arm to the rhythm

For that moment,
Something was different
For that moment,
She was neither
Serious nor sad

I was four
Yet sensed
How lucky I was to be small
"I'll be a child forever"
I promised myself

Now, in the heat of the summer
When the giant cottonwoods
Release their fragrant gift
I remember the promise.

School Days

Sometimes I dream of hallways
Lined with steel lockers and padlocks
I panic
Trying to recall a forgotten combination

I walk down the long hall
Conscious of self
Assessing others
Comparing

Linoleum tiled classrooms
Aroma of chalk, disinfectant
Cheap perfume
And chewing gum

There are no guns or switchblades here
Only a balding principal with a paddle
And a bunch of kids
Practicing to be grown up.

Rite of Passage

Something wet
An unfamiliar cramp
Takes my breath away

I slip secretly out of history class
Into a deserted hall
And push open the heavy door
That says "Girls"

Steel stalls line
White walls
I know what will happen next
It's my turn to put
A dime in the machine
I'd seen others use

I stuff the money in
And grab the box

No celebration
No rite of passage ceremony
For me
Only the Kotex machine
And an empty restroom
Share my secret.

Young Maiden

She offered him her heart
On a platter of innocence
He took it tenderly at first
Then greedily consumed it

Hormones raging
You cannot blame him
After a while he moved on
To feast upon another

Some say when a limb is severed
You grow a phantom appendage
Time did not heal
The young maiden

Though a phantom heart grew
In the cavity of what was
Her heart could feel pain and joy
Yet never did it beat quite the same.

A Sidewalk Game

While taking a stroll one summer day
I saw two little boys lost in play

They sat together on the sidewalk
Enjoying their day with laughter and talk
Facing each other playing a card game
Thinking not of fortune or fame

Deep in their thoughts, they noticed not I
I wanted to stay, but left with a sigh
For I'm grownup and must conform
To adult ways accepting the norm

In the next moment, I laughed at my mind
Soul is a child rules cannot bind

Years may have passed, yet I'm still the same
My heart still longs for a sidewalk game.

Jackpot Fever

I heard that the sun rose this morning
Yet little did I care
I was busy feeding the slot machine
His greenback breakfast fare

He's hungry today, sucking up bills
Releasing just a few
Two for twenty, five for fifteen
Yet my love for him stays true

I'm mesmerized by his promise
Of wealth and freedom from strife
I visualize a whopping win
Enough to change my life

To heck with food and sightseeing
The Grand Canyon is no big deal
Sedona's red rocks are just passé
Next to this thrill I feel

People say there's karma to pay
When I win the big jackpot
After I've spent my last dollar
Perhaps I'll give that some thought.

Cats- A- Plenty

I'm blessed with cats a-plenty,
As many as I can find
I love them each to pieces,
I'm not the monogamous kind

No discrimination on my part,
Any feline will do
Affection, food, a cozy bed,
My furry friend's needs are few

Devon Rex, Siamese, or street cats
Are equally appealing
On a cold and desperate night
Their love is warm and healing

I don't mind when they sleep all day
Leaving stray fur here and there
All I ask is they please not spray
I think that's only fair.

Spell Breaker

Afraid to move, there is no motion
Longing for a magic potion
To break this spell I am under
Is there hope for me, I wonder?

Like a statue, I sit and stare
At empty walls, I go nowhere
Thoughts play tricks, I am depressed
My love of life has been suppressed

Then suddenly, I feel her fur
And in my ear I hear a purr
A song of love she does impart
To gently wake my sleeping heart.

Between

Somewhere between hope and despair
Elation and depression
Exists a middle path
Of surrender and acceptance

A place of peace
Where the gentle breeze of eternity blows
And soul resides in perfection
How could it be less?

Morning Bird

I was basking in the slumber
Of night's repose
When morning bird appeared
And threatened to impose
In the shadows of a dream
His singing beckoned me
Calling me to earth
When I longed to be free

To explore and create
Beyond all space and time
In kaleidoscopic worlds
Limitless, sublime

Cease your revelry, I begged
I must prolong this night
For dawn will soon arrive
To end my dreamtime flight

For a time, I lingered
In the place where worlds combine
Which was true reality?
Both earth and dreams were mine

Then gently I returned
With the rising sun
As morning bird proclaimed
A new day had begun!

Since Graduation

Ten years later
At a social thing called reunion
We stare at each other like a roadside attraction
Assessing classmates
For signs of success
And agedness
Remembering the sweet illusion
Of innocence
That united us
When we walked, pranced, and flirted
Down the halls
Of our alma mater

With dreams in our pockets
Of the freedom residing
Just beyond the classroom door

Wishing away our days of youth
Willing to trade them
For a diploma

And tonight,
Gathered together once again
We are still united
Because we know now
In our weary but still hopeful hearts
Freedom was not free.

Midlife

Midlife is
The afternoon
You'd better hurry
For soon night falls

Youth is spent
Choices fade like
Smoke in the wind
Life is a half eaten chocolate cake

The tempo quickens
Where is love?
Sift the superficial
From the truth

Forgive yourself
For precious time wasted
Don't look back
There is no future in the past

A reality check
What have I accomplished?
And still need to do?
Thank God there's still time to dream.

The Thief

Just as you settle down
To reap the rewards of
Well-earned wisdom...
Symptoms appear

They batter your body
Plunder your psyche
Shake your spirit
And strip your joy

Yet you go through the motions
Faking sunshine and smiles
To prolong the illusion
That nothing has changed

A thief has stolen
Your eternal youth
And the loss is mourned
With every hot flash

Daring not to speak of the crime
You wonder, as you sweat,
If anyone notices
You've been robbed.

The Bathroom Mirror

Standing before the bathroom mirror
As I have done throughout each year
Carefully inspecting my reflection
Searching for an imperfection

This old mirror has never been kind
Still I keep looking, hoping to find
An image of beauty, uniquely mine
The perfect face, flawless and fine

Years have passed and now I see
A stranger staring back at me
Transformations taking place
A woman with an unknown face

Yet deep within familiar eyes
Lies ageless wisdom in disguise
Hidden beneath yesterday's grandeur
Now resides a timeless treasure

A rose in bloom, a loving heart
I wish I'd known from the start
I could be free of this mirror's gauge
Of beauty and worth, whatever my age.

Autumn

Summer silently slips away
Autumn settles in
Claiming its rightful place
In the everlasting cycle

An in-between kind of season
Lingering in the space
Of what was
And what will be

Summer is our youth
Autumn is letting go
Shedding golden leaves as
We cling to remembrances of days gone by

Of birth and growth
Love and grief
Memories that sustain the soul
On its eternal journey

Harvest time
A time of reflection and gratitude
The wise prepare
For the silver winter ahead.

Through the Lens

Holding you again
Like a long lost friend
Peering through your lens
At a speck of eternity
As a tiny voice whispers
"Look closer"

Witness the little things
Which are really the big things
Simple ceremonies

A holiday dinner, a soccer game
A birthday, memorial service
Or a visit from Aunt Kay
All the firsts
All the lasts

"Smile!" I say
The artist in me seizes the moment
And my finger moves
Click!
Freezing the image
On film for a time
Yet imprinted on my heart forever.

The Key

The key for today
Lies hidden in the past
Find it and unlock the door
To yourself

For you are the result of
Generations of others
That came before

Ancestors that walked and talked
Suffered and celebrated
Loved and hated
Gave birth and buried loved ones
Fought battles
Wept tears of joy and despair
Bled to death
Patched themselves up, healed, and went on

Why bother with the past?
Your blood is their blood
You are not alone
Connected
Call upon them to help you
Walk beside you
And give to you the wisdom
Only time imparts.

Voice of the Heart

The voice of the heart
Is silence
Yet it demands to be heard
So we speak
Choosing words carefully
Knowing all along
Symbols of script and sound
Fall short
Diluting and obscuring
Our Truth.
The words
Are like shadows
Compromising detail, color, and form
Only suggesting
Not reflecting
The riches
Within.

Suddenly

It was Christmas Day
When Normal went away
I stood alone
Watching in horror
As a heavy steel door
Appeared without warning
Slamming shut
My world, my birthright

Now, occasionally
A bit of fresh wind blows in
From around the cracks
And sweet muffled sounds
Of life tease my ears
Reminding me of before

How foolishly I assumed
Life to be a deep well
Of health, vitality and choice
Blessings taken for granted
No more.

Color of Pain

Shards of brilliant light
Slashing tissue and bone
Screaming, demanding
"Listen to me!"

Relentless
Unceasing
Minutes drag into hours
Hours into days

In fevered anguish
A plea to the Universe
For the magic pill
Or bucket of water
To extinguish the flames

Yet there's no escape from this
Red hot
Trial by fire.

Passing Show

Brown bird outside my window
How I envy you today
In the dead of winter
You sing though skies are gray

Where does your song come from?
I can only cry
For I am weak and cannot dance
Yet easily you fly

Then I heard a whisper
"It's just a passing show!
Brown bird celebrates his life
But soon, he too, must go."

Suddenly, I wasn't alone
In my desperate state
I knew in time we all depart
To stand at heaven's gate.

Remorse

Fly no more little bird
Feathers plucked mercilessly
Lay in still repose

Easy prey, this trusting soul
Lured in for an quick meal
His last supper
At the bird seed buffet

Was it a cagey cat?
A hungry hawk?

Tufts of brown plumage
Lay scattered at my feet
A downy memorial

Some say it's the circle of life
And survival of the fittest
Yet, if it weren't for
My helping hands
Would he be flying free?

Hope

I watched my mother
Carefully washing the fresh blueberries.
"These are for your dad," she said.

Rinsing, sorting and freezing berries
As he lay in intensive care,
Machines and medicine keeping him alive
For another day.

I said nothing,
Just nodded my head and thought,
"Yes, Dad loves these."

Grace

25

*Grace lives
In the subtle space between.*

*'Tween the musical notes
That lift our hearts to heaven,*

*And in the space
Within each breath*

*That sustains our body
On earth.*

Sunrise Mission

Just in time
For the morning show
Velvet fog fades with the rising sun
Golden rays
Shoot out from the fireball
And shimmer across the bay
Gulls cry out their high-pitched
"Scree! Scree!"
Dipping and circling
Riding the winds of change
I dare to walk alone
With a camera, a hat, and frozen fingers
Lost in "the zone"
Zooming in, tracking the loveliness
Rapid-fire shots
Moments are captured
Digitalized, printed and framed
To bring you along
Breathe salt air
Make footprints in wet sand
Pocket an agate and a clam shell
As waves pound the shoreline
In perfect rhythm.

A Little Bit of Crazy

On a snowy winter morn
Before the rising sun and songs of birds
While others slumber and coffee brews
Something supersedes breakfast
Comfort and climate
A call
To capture in digital detail
Nature's awakening
There's a little bit of crazy
In those crack of dawn photographers
With bed head hair
Layers of mismatched clothing
Wool caps, fingerless gloves
Easing winter's bite
Scanning the horizon, listening
With thoughts of light and shutter speed
Stealthy, determined, alert creatures
With rosy frozen faces
Lugging hefty telephoto lenses
We tell ourselves
It's all worth it
Crazy is underrated!

Time Capsule

It's three in the morning
Every quarter hour the mantle clock chimes
I should be asleep
But tonight feels like a gift I don't want to let go of
I'm sleeping in my old room
Who gets to do that?
Who gets to go home as a senior citizen
And sleep in their childhood bed?

Where I had the chicken pox, growing pains
And pneumonia so bad I floated out of my body

Gone is the wood dresser adorned with
Sea shells and ceramic Siamese cats
And the ballerina jewelry box
Nested on Grandma's lace doily

The walls are still pale yellow
A flower painting has long replaced
My bulletin board
The heartbeat of a young life
Sacred scraps of paper thumb-tacked to it
Postings that evolved with age

This little room
Where fleeting hours of childhood were spent
Kneeling on a waxed hardwood floor
In an innocent haze

Bent over Barbie dolls
Playing scratched vinyl records
On a 1950's phonograph

A world where
Imagination was real and nectar for soul
And the future was far away

I look up
The star- studded glass light fixture still hangs there
It would be called retro today

Each night, I'd stare at that light and know
This is my room, my light
As a kid, few things under your parents roof
Are really yours
But this, I knew, was mine

Now, here I am
A wife, mother, grandma,
Author, photographer
And survivor of life

But in this time capsule, I am none of those things
My mom taps on the door and whispers,
"Are you ok?"

I wonder...

Does she know in this room I am still eight years old?

Winter's Gift

Aged fingers trace
Crystalline patterns of window frost
As cotton-candy snowflakes
Dance upon the wind

Like the snow covered trees
She rests in well-earned dormancy
A lifetime of seeds have been planted
To bloom in latter days

A snowy down comforter blankets the earth
Tucking it in for a season's repose
She stands alone on her old wooden porch
Beholding winter's gift

Timeless white frosting
A Christmas card portrait
Of pristine innocence
The hush of infinity frozen in place

In the stillness of the moment
She touches the eternal
And her heart remembers
Serenity.

Blessed Sunlight

Farewell frigid winter
And days of dark despair
When frail elders perished
You did not seem to care

Youth survived and blossomed
And filled their time with play
While others simply counted
Each passing dreary day

Returning birds confirm
The promise of rebirth
A long awaited sun
Now thaws a frozen earth

Winter days behind us
Old Sol's a welcome sight
Nature's atonement is
A gift of blessed light.

Soul

Soul is the software
That slips into the hardware
At birth
A perfect union

Powered by
The omnipresent Universal Server

A full-service plan
Granted by grace
And extending until
Mission fulfilled.

Another Springtime

It's now another springtime
As she looks into the mirror
That shows so many seasons
And days of yesteryear

The birds outside are singing
Songs she's heard before
How many years, she wonders
Will spring knock at her door?

It's now another springtime
The world outside is new
She knows that she is aging
And only passing through

An inner voice is whispering
"Your time is almost here"
With memories of love inside
She has but little fear

It's now another springtime
With promises to be
For her it is the season
When love will set her free.

A Note from Sally

Dear Poetry Lover,

Your feedback means a lot to me. If you enjoyed reading my poetry, I'd love to hear from you.

Please leave a review on Amazon, and if you'd like to say hello, you can contact me at: www.sallyharrisbooks.com/contact.

Photo by Todd Katke

Sally M. Harris is a nationally recognized children's book author, poet and inspirational writer. She's also an award winning nature photographer, specializing in bird photography. Ideas for writing usually come to her while dreaming or spending time in nature. Her personal mission is to open the hearts of many with words, stories, and photography. Sally lives on the Olympic Peninsula and is often inspired by the nearby snow-capped mountains and ocean.

www.ingramcontent.com/pod-product-compliance
Lightning Source LLC
Chambersburg PA
CBHW040116150726
48005CB00013B/1733